GEORGE WASHINGTON'S WARS

WITH HIS SLAVE, ONA JUDGE

by

James William Chichetto

Also by James Wm. Chichetto

STONES, A LITANY

DIALOGUE: EMILY DICKINSON AND

      CHRISTOPHER CAULDWELL

GILGAMESH AND OTHER POEMS

VICTIMS

HOMAGE TO FATHER EDWARD SORIN, 1ST ED.

HOMAGE TO FATHER EDWARD SORIN, 2ND ED.

RECKONING GENOCIDE

THE DREAM OF NORUMBEGA, Books I, II, III, IV

BLOOD ACCOUNTS

In token of my highest regard for his
Genius, this book is inscribed
to Robert Peters (1924-2014), poet,
scholar, critic, playwright, editor, friend,
and creator of the "voice portrait."

and

to Fannie Lou Hamer (1917-1977)
Pacifist, Rights Activist
and extraordinary woman of faith

Special thanks to Paul Trachtenberg; Claudia Buckholts
and Thomas Glannon; Kevin Spicer, CSC; James
Fenstermaker, CSC; John Denning, CSC;
Bryan Williams, C.S.C.; Frank and Dale Chichetto;
William and Christine Sennett; Brain and Laurie
Doherty; Judith Sughrue; Brian Healy;
Warren Dahlin; and Mary Ann Payne,
National Endowment for the Humanities.

"Every step of progress which the world has made
has been from scaffold to scaffold,
and from stake to stake."

Wendell Philips, Abolitionist

"And was the holy Lamb of God…seen?"

William Blake's "Jerusalem"

"In general, the dear black people, that profess
Religion, are much more engaged [in faith]
than the Whites."

William Spencer, Methodist

"That spirit of freedom, which at the
commencement of this contest would have gladly
sacrificed everything to the attainment of its object,
has long since subsided and every selfish
passion has taken over."

George Washington
Washington to Henry Laurens, 1779

"Nations [have] long dreamt for their national unity
In some common fund of religious ideas."

Ernest Barker, political scientist

"Their griefs [of slaves] are transient…are less felt,
and sooner forgotten."

Thomas Jefferson

"Even in our sleep, pain which cannot forget falls
drop by drop upon the heart, until, in our own
despair, against our will, comes wisdom through
the awful grace of God.'

> Robert F. Kennedy, quoting Aeschylus, at
> Rev. Martin Luther King's funeral.

"Sin shall be inevitable, but all shall be well.
And all manner of things shall be well."

> Julian of Norwich, Catholic mystic.

"He hath loosed the fateful lightning
        of His terrible swift sword."

> Julia Ward Howe
> BATTLE HYMN OF THE REPUBLIC

"Mr. Humphrey, what I really want is the immediate
establishment of God's kingdom here on earth."

> Fannie Lou Hamer, Civil Rights Pacifist in her
> answer to Vice President-elect H. Humphrey's
> question at the Democratic Convention,
> 1964: "Mrs. Hamer, what do you really want?"

Ona judge's Prologue:

O what say ye, Winfield of Dinwiddie,
Kindred Spirit of war-smarted Smith
Amongst those who are dead?
When Memory of Youth lurks red,
It's full of mischief, unrest,
Getting drunk on its head.
But under Elijah's call
Battles beckon us all
Betwixt grit and fear
Toward rivers that flow like blood
Until caught in the swirl
Of a darker river's flood.

There's a lot to say of war, of battles,
Appointing weight to ventures,
Deeds of one sort or another
Fraught with dangers.
Yet is that what we're about,
To make Thermopylae true,
The sound of picks and shovels
As if gut-wrenching new?
But let's begin
From depths of the past
Where one truth ripens,
Crueler than the last.

Washington:

There's no room for lies here under April's sun,
Nor perch for fools with grease-fouled tongues!
But brassy I'll start whatever the remarks as the
Sun struts over the hill with the day's good will.
But take not my dare to a whipping post
To labor Job with hope or Judas from despair....
I 'm my brother's keeper
                          but like the peal of thunder.

Ona Judge:

Yes, yes Washington! No conscience steals
Your sleep, nor preys on heart to stir our feet!
You see with a second eye
                          each stalk and leaf.

Washington:

My claims ought be more modest: Grandson, great
Of a planter— blood-mouthed he, un-puffed, earnest,
A bribe to his betters; whose soles on the planks
Of docks stalked fretting as he walked long before
Quitting England and the fuss of that land....
Aye, ranks before me will parade, piping of him
And kin — off like the wind in the sun's fat blaze! To
Eclipse a Past he came for eye-stunned change!

Ona Judge:

Chesapeake Colonies! Indentured drudges
Blistered, broken! Destitute, scummy,
Cropped for work! Laborer servants!
But none of this in Washington's circle!
His kin had a free arrival, yes,
With a head start for survival!
No broken out of captivity for them!
No remote sunset, red-frosted,
Quenched by candle-dark!
No under their hearts' death-drawers of dirt,
Nor spitting into rivers hurt!

Washington:

At eleven, my mother's widowed! Doubts shoot
Up to the sky then; panic tips the heart and soul
As if in the midst of new things and old.
But I'm not one postponing words of beggary here
For a brother to pass closer to him, tighter, like
A root shock-pried new. I learn that Fortune waits
Up the road a bit, bled-out from behind some
Surveyor's rule, whose dirt-veined heart drifts West.

Ona Judge:

Good Lawrence at Belvoir, overseer! Mate of
Ann Fairfax! Wealth beyond axe with whip
And lash! We figured that! Lawrence, who
Overshadows loss! Kiss him, good sir,
As good fortune occurs!

Washington:

Such is my fate from the beginning, aye,
Hustling self to route Etiquette, learn right
Manners betwixt deer-track spotting and texts
At night. O the cradled woods of Virginia and
Beyond, lands vendible, coined with scant
Reflection except for battles won by yeomen
Muscle! Yet this land is mine, laudable to bear
An earlier hour with ready laughter, thorny
Snicker; but the grit on my teeth pricks me to
Leap – aye to chase all manner of things, then
Close the circle on tribes 'ere some Frenchman
Bronzed with fever puts up his thumb! My heart
Crackles on for this early, intent and edgy, before
Sentiments in battles spill on some goblin hill out
West. What is it that I fear? Nothing except
The wrong gesture or word to betray my wit,
Indict my culture, cut me from my betters.
I know red-eyed that Forces change, roll aloft
Like moon-washed tides ebbing, baring reef,
Only again to swell, shift, climb anew, then shrink.
But life sulks testy here, stirring wild to a mutinied
West with old rules new to grip as if for greater
Benefit. Light's a God-shadow, scolds Plato,
And in that shade we change, rough-hewn
Hyperions, change utterly to friend or foe. But
Time yet chases me with auguries
Bidding me where it please.

Ona Judge sings:

America! Therein lies your skill,
Red-faced Washington —
Self-defined to hold the pull of plenty
Rolled in blood!
We are grateful!

Washington:

The Grand Divider of events goads me, heckles
My soul to one-voiced become unbent; but
None can shape that will. Others choke on lofty
Words as if to raise some blizzard wind so near as
To the past with mystic dates. But I learn young
To mold steel to consequence. The Great
Dispenser yields sense to those who siphon it as
He rolls paths our way on a good day. But again
I digress from childhood, whose flaws I cannot
Omit behind Virginia's good will and merriment.
In order to blink forward I must hie backwards,
Sun-scrubbed; hie on trails dense-packed,
Dazzled by inkling hearts at doors held more
Open than not, beyond cart-rut paths, trees
Hacked, and fields scorched black. I grow up
In advance of that direction,
Clutching a shrieking gun.

Ona Judge:

But America, this be you
With nothing but the name Pilgrim o'er the land
In Native hands.
He stretches to shine bright beyond borders!
Aye, he stretches like a surveyor wrapped in fir,
America's heir!

Ona Judge:

O what would old Franklin say
To kinsmen kind,
Who can't be rooked
On work-dotted lines
To note the human heart,
Its riddle and mystery
With tackle on back
For savagery?

O Franklin, Franklin,
Set our Washington right!
"Blows must decide"
The coming fight!

See, see, see the coming tide!

To turn round is right,
Cruel as kind!
Laid in milky whiteness
No Washington's blind
So bodied in mind!
What's held on the line? On paper?
Just the land he was after, creek-bed and river.

Ona Judge:

He played as his forefathers played
Abetted by fortune, estate,
Ambition jointed by pain
As farmers spilled the same blood
Bashing Native brains.

It was as if all the dead broke into words
When they won at Yorktown,
Their invisible hands beating the earth
As if to hoist on air a curse on England
For their deaths and suffering.

Enough, enough, I hear!
We are barely ahead
On this darkened slope
With breath drooling
As if with drafts, globs of ink
On a death-heavy air!
Let him speak on his own ground
Among kinsmen in town
To pull all boasting down!

Washington:

And dance, who can slight dance or bite breath
Crackling with strength, vigor? The surfeit of it all
In polite society for one in command goads those
Who break to prize you, or come round in size to
Jiggle you gentry! And what's the warrant that
Good Fortune comes to me? The light heart of
Virginians! Easy that grand heart imparts the
Best to a good dancer!
And if, too, he's clever, honest – that'll do!

Ona Judge:

Dance, reel, Washington, loose-legged
Under the blue skies' wind! Dance with brother's
Fiddle! Howl out brains with ambition, served up
With daybreak notes and wingbeat hope!

And the overseer's whip! Is Austin watching
With stoic lip we slaves, or ache that's missed
At work camp shifts?

Washington:

Aye, my schooling's as bereft, awry, but manners
Resurrect in me the best primers yet! The 100 RULES
I repeat over and again, with pine-flecked back
Against chair or rail, so long as it strains the mind as
Forward, then backwards as if on some menaced
Spot outdoors! How I labor the right word to fit, the
Apt phrase to the void of talk whether in yard, on
Street walks or at table, putting meat to my lips! But
I learn, cocked and sleek in town, to get the Rules
Down. I learn to write in plain-edged lines, but with
Forge of ready belief as if on eagle's wings, swift
And fleet. I want to soar inwards as at a distance
And grow, however willful my show, as if scarcely
I bear a sixth sense or for some captious AIM was
Sent. Foolish it seems, I know, on this smoke-filled
Ground, born of circumstance cut down, a dazzled
Soul; but in pastures of planters, deeds stalk the
Ghosts of emperors.

Ona Judge:

Our lives matter, too, but where's my father?
I know a skeleton from a ghost,
The moon on a window pane.
Both seem white in wasted smoke.

Washington:

I know mine and mine know
Me, chides the Lord in Scripture. I, too, know such
As if in sleep or in dreams saddled to a steed of
Never-resting consciousness or in awkward
Reverence, to think what I must do! Something
Burns true in me, aye, pure, something rough-cast
I seize upon with both hands knowing right friends
Will stand by me year after year, vigilant, watchful
With iron will! Such are my thoughts some days as if
On the cusp of surety, thinking past
Hot-blood dreams, dance scores, steps of a maid
Toward me. I know the risks at times like these—
The perils one takes to dot victory— of leaps too
Quickly sprung. But when battles flaunt drops
Worse than feet can reach, depths where
Demons meet, I cloak with Wisdom my
Thoughts for sure Providence and cold sense.

Ona Judge:

Nothing! You can't hear me, sir.
But I swim by you as if from within myself
Until your sunken eyes
Retain the gem-hard ache
Of our passage upward.

Washington:

So, too, I catch things as surveyor, scrawling what
I know of these lands as if debts in old ledgers,
Cut by farm-hands: I learn accountings are
Titled, private, the King's and the elite's; that
Land's a compulsion leased to folks; that tracts
Aren't skimmed but surveyed; that miles like
Words are yoked to paper; that dearth is
Trade-made to make excess scarcer; that land
Doesn't breathe unless kings stir; off maps,
Tis but a specter. But ambition never jades me
Stalking a Future — the distemper of land,
The gravity of record, my family's score,
My own command on a fence or 'round
Some stretch of ground, with grasslands veined
Best in all manner of stock— soiling, hawking
What I get for profit; cold-blooded with zeal to
Fritter boyish need! That zeal I take with me each
Sunbaked day! Aye, its grunting weight conferred
I feel in courtyard or on bloody field alike
To crush what I strike.

Ona Judge:

Thrifty Washington! Wadding lands, dreams,
Bare-headed! Rigged out in boots, sunburnt,
Heavy-eyed to wipe clean the slate, pure as
A knife's heart! That's America, sir, over trenches
Space-rich, over crop and field sun-cracked on
Map-dreams predestined, with Providence blazing
Down reticent, fir-green! Everything for the taking!

Washington:

Good Lawrence lauds me best! Sibling with whom I
Blend, free of circumstance, un-vexed as if under
Heaven's judgment; he who let me learn quick his
Meanly woes — his deeds my rule in gold!
How mighty be that presence, aye, that counsel,
His copy and sense! I grip that honor as with a son's
Hand; his nature as with a slave's palm, a
Heart-breadth to match his calm, clench it panting
As if to stand equal to his reign lenient as though
A rule of heart. But nights I fret, how can I excel
Madam? Mind what mettle she has over my own?
Praise a brother's rank to show myself swifter,
On equal footing? Her hardiness, raw sense always
Meant more to me than any hayseed cousin's or
Mate's wit, boisterous to win merit, incite a
Riot or two! Her intent always pricks me, however
Stone-hard I stray or scarce can accept it.
Thus I gain to abide by her as one 'round a sire.
Yet I'm never enough in my deed-forged station!
Maybe weightier she sees more stuff in me, some
Raw haven where Europe ends, full of heart-felt
Traits, features that strike her safe: — ruddy veins of
Discipline firm, swollen hard within that will take me
Further in ambition—though humbly? But am I free
Full tide to chide aloud, mutter ambition, pursue
Ventures in clock-work shifts, for risk,
Free of her reach?

Ona Judge:

Go easy on her—
Upright, selective, alone—
Racing before a rebuke
Or after one
To be good.
Perhaps pious she's more
Smooth-skinned than her iron will,
As if weighing an uncertain son
All too weak to become a name,
To concede him her virtue?
Her name is Mary Ball Washington,
Born in 1708.
Sit alone with her if you will
From opposite ends of a hall;
From all her burdens she speaks:
'My inner persistence makes
For frozen ground!
But I know my son,
The dexterity of his pride within,
The aspiration rising to his lips….
When sun sinks meadowsweet
I've these mute principles,
As if from under worn sheets,
To hold senses still.'

Washington:

'I know not!' I think this in resolution to her presence.
But what else upon me weighs so to blunt that sense?
I'm so much her replica, lion-mettled, unbent; yet
When dawn wakes me, ne'er so mindful, so free!
But I gain as I go along with life's wagers ahead
To temper the ire bred as if on a march singly long
As heart stirs to raptures within. But imagine to her
Wonder when I'm called up by Fairfax: a rookie
Surveyor at seventeen! A stunning task at any age,
The youngest in history to test skills in Culpeper,
Then to Shenandoah as if to the bowels of some
Country delinquent to be. In resolution mute, I
Whistle to the sun, hoping daily to lay up money,
Aye, sheaves of it, far and near,
With spring scarcely here.

Ona Judge:

We are, then we aren't in this country, so new
To make an end, so bound to time, ox-carts
And bled hearts. We are broken off by show
Of spring, rattling thunder!
Have you something more sunk in the head
That anger keeps and autumn sheds?

Ona Judge:

Ever wonder about sage Homer
Who fretted how the Greeks fought,
Whose oars beat deadly against the Waves
But deadlier in men's hearts?

His lines pelted the weak and strong;
His blood-choked words were dark,
As if sprawled on a sheep skin scroll
Like blood on a dog's back.

Of tribulations he wrote,
Whose heroes cut each other's throats.
Hector's dragged behind a chariot
Like a doll on Homer's rope.

Blood looked at Homer like water,
Like every murder,
The flow of Abel's blood.
Nothing could freeze that river
Bronzed by weed and mud.

Ona Judge on reflection:

That's no way to treat Homer, men say—
To pluck his scruffy beard,
His posthumous face
Worn fifty years
With Trojan song on tongue
That clings to Priam's sons
And eats away his tunes
On hurried drums!

O the gun, the gun of darkness!
The face of mercy, too!
The battlefield of song
That melodies be true!
The race for those swift on foot
Before the cap of winter!
And behold the vanquished soldier
Shot by frightened killers!

War's force to Homer – murderous —
Soldiers hewn from pate to groin.
And if with palm undone,
Havoc by another comes —
The war-tormented son's,
Until the slaughter's done.

Ona Judge:

O Washington! America's son! You come
No stranger, your sequent account! We hear
Your gallop, your hoof-measured pace!
We turn to you, your blood-bound road!
No journey of Aeneid's as bold!

But we bear grief, too,
To adjust to earth,
To shout our best
Our curse of words.
And don't tell us of life, of death
Grazed against nakedness
Carved on skeleton heaps
To erase sleep.
Oh ye whitened sepulchers
Behind a shack raping her
No nuptial scream no puppet stir
Squeezed in the grip of night
To erase century light!
We have borne our grief
That oceans keep
Where bodies roll and plead for sleep.

Washington:

All this, I think, in disbelief as acres more I align to
Name; my shrill thoughts sun-streaked, hot to
Wide-armed claims! In all, two thousand, three
Hundred fifteen acres gained! Like a bee in
Sloping flower I reel, culling ascendency –
The pine for land, soil; not feigning from behind
Some colleague's fence nights, as with scorned
Regret, staging defense for yielding naught my
Suited hand — with mind, heart to stanch loss,
And faith, apt and lost!
But loss in another way I feel, feeble-limbed, as if
Wrought by things I flee: the grief-struck days
Clouding me, so storm-dark, desperate!
My task's to whisk death from sickness,
The bare-backed rounds it makes, as Lawrence
Worsens! Impatient, we sail to England first as if
For remedy; his tuberculosis needing respite,
Rest, a different country's test. But England's
Fog holds no sun; as if condemned, we leave.
In this with hearts numb, shrunk but tenacious,
Hopeful, firm-set, expectant as brothers, friends —
We're coaxed by love. Is this what we discover?
A citizen figure half-dead, so believed, though not
Beyond respite (—his trust of reprieve as if in sight).
Yet so much of this is ear-fed through hearsay,
Rumor, the mechanisms of fear, tugging doubt
As in not a calloused few. And grieved I'm left,
As if rebuking heart against bouts of worse reports.

Washington:

After this, it's off to Barbados, a tropical warmth
At sea, a passage of thirty-seven days through
Rain and breeze. Hope's so round-eyed then,
As if wind-muscled within to the nth degree.
Dear Lawrence, dead-eyed, weaker, owns no
Sense of a future – the sights, the sounds of the
Island, the littered cane, the fat beets, the yams
I like. But soon stricken I'm with pox sores, whose
Seams brandish worse scars. But travel's useless
Still! No wave-deafening air can rouse him, make
Him less ill, nor island check his end.
Later in Bermuda he dies, dies — is shut off, closed
With those Spirits in that Great, Dark Silence!
O Lord, Lord, to what is best in me he spoke
To lure a bolder hope! He was ever my counselor,
Mentor, father fixed on my future, that sphere to
Expand, to strive for and find deep within the mind.
The earth writhes, twists as if from within, pants
In me, then readies still as I trudge from grave.
No gauze balms eyes afflicted, nor feelings aid
As to shut down this sadness. In this probation
I should blessed feel as if to take the way home
For his goodness alone. But I grieve within,
Sink as to the bones, make death seem my own
Having so kept to him. Death snatched my brother
As to choke our future.

Ona Judge:

Walk, walk and learn that already death has come!
No one escapes.

Washington:

But what an Autumn, appalling still,
As if lengthened under grief
That I haste to!
Yet the years chastened leap!
When spirits lie beaten
They lie not dead,
But rave at will,
As if reaching through steel,
To gain hold
Of the punished living.
But excess of grief
The speedy brain impedes.
What more can I do as surveyor
I'll face as soldier.
And this I do before
My twenty-first birthday!
Can one go wrong, robed
As for war and high-placed praise?
I'm district adjutant,
As if part of a throbbing firmament,
The sun-streaked Crown,
Goading it to stretch round
Further, engird the whole continent!
A major, ripening victories   ,
In my head, aye, strange matters, fancies,
'Ere to war sent!
This am I – untroubled, incorporate to braggart-wisdom,
Piling triumphs abstract, forebodings, one by one.

Washington:

Now I'm bustling, sun-soaked with a stint,
An anointed task, a chore for Dinwiddie —
Mounting horse o'er graveled roads, through
Woods to sound the enemy,
Speed for King a message.
I'm wedged
Inside a cleft of sorts, a bull-dozed post
Where wars end, as if to rush against bug-eyed
Hosts, doomed with fate in hand.
Perhaps this triumph's too bold, — aye, too strong
As if for those who guard Eden, unarmed;
But I'm young with groundling plans
As if pitched into a Punic venture,
Boot-kicked by nature.   *Ona Judge:*
Bullets! I hear them still,
The crackle of sound   *War with the French as*
As if teasing Sibyl's spell: *though the whole war*
My fighter's arm   *held only him,*
Saber-like, husky   *harnessed to a hymn!*
Dodging their mortal breeze,
The Frenchman's duty
To kill me!
Say what you will of bravery,
Fortune linked to fate's call
That hustles the soul and kindles
Silken its embers for some crueler century!
But my axe will post its mark
However grave the thought!

Washington:

Looking back on Half King —
The savage betrayals, the bravery of Gist,
The fiery insects stinging,
The slaughter, men sunk murderous by hatchets,
The French scalps
Concluded, strung like dry tokens,
My prudent measures taken
At the Jumonville event —
Of these all, lean truths are told
As if by slant; libels by degree,
Strung-out as if by throe
To crack the soul.
But nothing made me suffer
To stick to one master.
The Crown always I've merited; the King
Spoke where I breathed
As if at the back of the ears,
Brassy free!
It was that always,
Though the smut of Half King's ways,
His speech flouting me
Hurried too cruelly.
I took upon myself 'to command
Them as slaves,' he claims
With nothing but my name
Linked as if to piddling land.
The Fort was 'a little thing
Upon the meadow,' aye, a trifling?

Washington:

Fort Necessity the savage
Never got! Its blood-soaked dirt
We gave way
To the pitiless French first!
How we suffered from dense fire,
As if from every rising and tree;
Rain-drenched, leaning on one another,
We lay in mud, smothered
As they butchered every dog,
Cow, and horse to the river!
The ground grew fat from the blubber,
The knotted joints chopped, hacked off
To score a victory!
This led to slurs against me.
But blame, what's blame to boldness!
Who dares, must risk a fall!
Fortune favors us!
My loss reached all
As one who to a fear-gutted front,
Stepped as if in a moment's heat
And learned from War
Caesar's chores.
Have I regrets to hurl for this debacle?
That I was made assassin
Will not drown the sin!
But I'm innocent of this swill
Heaped on me. I do say
This and aver it to this day!

Washington:

I killed no Jumonville in that slaughter!
Half King led both spoilers and killers! As
Mutineers they axed prey before fright-plugged
Eyes, filling the air with cries. I laid low in shock,
Despaired, safe from keen-edged hatchets,
As if from them apart, stranded, sovereign in a
Trench. Without strength enough to hold them,
I gripped in fist my gun. But the House of Burgesses,
Later — through autumn — rallied for me as if in apt
Words ready, aye, fitted to me by McKay for this
Gallant effort in defense of country!
In counsel, they judged one can't for long be
Charged unjustly, cudgeled — beat from within;
And what was amiss or stripped bare of victory
Was not to be my fault or reckoned so.

Ona Judge:

Who strikes with tongue? A grass-sucked sky does
That wastes the sun. So play courage to death
With rebel breath! Tie wolves by the neck!
Beat their flesh a knotted wreck!
Say it for us all! We take freedom with your shouts
Equally bloody to cross us out!

Washington:

But frightened, held back, I know my weakness
Having given face to war;
Yet know, too, the unrest
To bear no arms the more.
I need no mad-eyed word
To incline my soul.
But I know already my choice,
As if overhearing a ghosted voice.
So in no time I stand dressed,
Ordering a new uniform
With gold loops and hat adorned
As if tailor-best.
What was once dear to me
Is ever dearer to be: to bear arms as soldier
However much blood's on one's coat fir
Or boots worn or toes swelled with corns.
Even in sleep I think this
With each brewed myth
I conjure up – however, screened with buttons
Shiny — as though a great shadow
Of fate on the wall can glimpse apace my ruin
Or palm! But in the night's coolness before rest
I know I'm blessed.

Ona Judge:

But slaves address you!, sir Here the bane be mightier
Than one so bold! 500,000 of us in the cold! We let you
Go for our victory! We gain in the end 'ere perishing.
Pick a virus, pick a trap! Pick a cell that houses rats!

Washington:

Then at twenty-two, I rent
Mount Vernon from Lawrence's widow,
Adjust murky claims, line up rights,
Rentals like nails in a row
To be duly hammered;
Under my order to trade and traffic, pinned
In exchange for tobacco, hogsheads
Each Christmas, are different crops, breads,
A barter as smooth as glass —
With eighteen slaves working hand
And limb as if for cut-priced land
And what I ask.
I attain status as though for myself
And airs of wealth.
But when Braddock
Drops anchor off Hampton Road,
I'm again forced loose, as if blood-hung, aye,
In shock as if on a mighty threshold
And rush to become soldier!
There are battles ahead more savage, stouter,
Crueler wars to endure, suffer
As if sweets in a mother's
Palm! With everything in place—
The mettle of strife,
Imperial quarrel, discord, hands on knives,
Muskets to coax a traitor, a parting face—
I race ahead in haste
To vie with fate!

Washington:

Yet Madam wants none of it,
Roused as if by the cry of my intent;
As if in pride — my conceit, up to the neck
In need of a bigger tent!
But, aye, I'm waiting as if to be born,
Befriend myself, favor me, veer west in song,
Mend more than my shirt;
Pull roots as if from blood-hot earth,
Plants of some wilderness
By wished-for mountains,
Absent borders,
Yielding to others much less.
But let me be – not so sure of every
Day, but to seize it freely!
'But you must stay,' she says.
No, I say, not nicking intent,
Impassioned eyes ablaze,
Appointing each word its weight.
'You owe your services here;
Youth obliges you to care
For your benefactors.
What of these obligations?
To expunge them now
Masks what a fugitive feels
Against good will.'
You must my task allow,
I say. My happiness
Is in this choice and wish.

Washington:

The particulars aren't known
But I say I know the way of war,
The route home
As if from within and trails afar.
My words rush both her eyes;
I measure them as if inside her head,
Mellowing the shock
Into a thousand thoughts.
After that, there's little talk.
In that instant, dusk comes on,
As if rushing her lawn.
I prepare to act,
Taking the trail to Braddock's
Camp without turning back.
Braddock! How does one deal
With a pith like Braddock
Whose king's regulars he feels
Grow mightier in attacks;
Who stakes Indians
Easy prey to a man,
Not shadows of different lengths,
Foes of hidden strength
In a forest where ambush
Across steep mountains
Can shrivel siege-guns
And make regulars limp.
But he listens not to reason
Nor wit in the end.

Washington:

And I'm just 'family,'
His private staff,
Someone illusory, at hand,
As on a fledgling's path,
With the regulars he commands
And mighty cannons.
What school-benched depths
Have I to ignore this?
But I write to mother:
'I'm happy in the General's family;
All is agreeable to me.
I'm ready for the campaign
To pronounce my name, aye, ours!
And as for butter, that too
Can't be had by army or you.'
When duty's laid out,
I see through the stretch of things,
The breadth of woods,
Of hills, winter to spring!
God tempers the night
To morning's light.
I'm not to lead Caesar's affairs
But strut in the rear
Of them, follow them
As Braddock commands.
How often iron-stiffed I've   .
Unearthed discontent
Among some, a rebuke of heart,
A news flash before shut eye
For having sunk too quiet
To the blare of giants.

Washington:

But under Braddock, I move about;
Am dispatched to Williamsburg
To rake up four thousand pounds,
But a detour I hatch for her –
For Sally, as if on certainty
To meet, perhaps in self-pity
To brew anew a strategy, a pretense
To gaze on her, as if to throw off the scent
Of my fixation, buoyed
Up by recklessness, yes,
But privilege, too, inside!
But am I some merchant's toy,
I think, as if a pawn not prized
Under playful eyes?
It's hard, so hard –
To sort beauty out, hers,
Though I'm headstrong, weak to be hurt,
As if sinking from within when drawn near.
I'm no child in this,
Put up by others to resist
Merit, approval,
Or to lie under some coaxed will.
But I beg for correspondence,
Partly pledged before,
As if in need of more
But caution less.
I'm Samson in this or
More fool take the hindmost than wit.

Washington:

Then off to Braddock's war
But not without a smaller war
Within to quell in this blade-flailing world,
A war Internal, cruel with sores —
Dysentery, with as much violence
And thrashing on one's sense
As any war braced, fought,
Lived out in one's guts!!
Try trekking in a wagon
With hemorrhoids swelled, thickened; forfeiting
Sleep, stripped bare inside from bleeding meat,
Drink, any morsel forsaken
Once put to the lips
Over hoof beats!
It's hell protruding
From within; and maddened I
Bent like a bow, brain-weary, aye, thin
With choked-up cries,
Being brave or a fool
Or by Juno's rule —
Cozened, possessed —
Wish to rush
The French from our lands!
Propped-up, steep like a corpse,
Upright, I bleed sap-like sores,
Believing victory at hand
Or if not, that I'd be cloaked,
Hooded as with hangman's cloth!

Washington:

This is how I enter the war —
With pads strapped to saddle
To ease the labor
Of battle –
My veins greatened
And I weakened
From blood-letting by big-jawed doctors
And their spell of orders!
But I'd rather take myself to be shot
First than not fight,
Evoke courage, might,
Valor, free a bolt
Or two on the enemy! So I begin to ford
The Monongahela with triumph
In mind, with Gage and Gates
Ahead, and me, by Braddock's side
Until I sense the mistake,
The shock inside,
The blunder unveiling, the bungling slip —
The war whoops, the paint and bullets
Flashing, then melting out of sight!
Soon it is too late to plan,
So pinned down had we become
With foes on their bellies sunk
Behind trees to a man.
I press Braddock to break his platoons,
Go native, act soon!

Washington:

But the propriety of it,
The jolt isn't felt until
Too late for the errant heart
To muster, coax the will
Of the fleeing English
Who whey-faced broke like sheep,
Ran like yelping hounds
On fox-held ground!
They fled to save their skins,
Crept into cradling woods,
Staggered, hid in willow beds
From wounded kin —
From Virginians bold who battled
As men and like men died.
How does one reach peace
On such a luckless day,
Come to hope inmost when
Beset by the play
Of cowards? But anew I turn
To battle, no longer seeing them
White-faced, sickly run. Two horses are
Shot from under me;
My need for pads, cushions
No longer felt, my boots,
Breeches in soot, mud
As if sunk beneath my gun.
That was a day trampled underfoot
By cowards, fleet on foot.

Washington:

And poor Braddock, felled
By a bullet gashing his arm,
His noble lung, goring!
His spirit at once strong, so strong
As if ahead of him, compassed on that bloody
Field, but now desperate in struggle, feeling
A kind of fury surface,
Stripping his victory first,
Then leaving little hope!
I was to carry out his orders—
Relay a message to Dunbar
For supplies, pound the route
Back on horseback for hours
Through blood-dark horror.
And horror it was, with shocking
Scenes of corpses rotting or rotted,
And the watchful cries of the maimed and dying
Not yct gathered!
O what a flesh-hacked scene to flee
Heightened to shreds in me,
As if holding captive within the murderous daylight
A blood-shrunk night!
The groans I heard and night-shrieks
Of men struck down
On skull-wrecked ground,
Lost faces to lost names!
Sleepless I rode from that defeat
Enraged as furor and disgust broke sleep.

Washington:

Later Braddock, dying, two miles
From the Great Meadows,
Hands me a sash and two pistols.
I feel the rush and flow
Of temper, his look, his racked face
As if cudgeled, disgraced,
His chest half-bared,
His sweat-spattered hair
Reared in idiot fashion
As one not of a great army
Or regimental breed
But as Crassus brought down!
Who is this under the scourge of death
After such carnage, waist-deep flesh?
He was beaten by his own, a trifling
Hem of men, cowardly
Blood-swollen regulars, languishing,
Weak-kneed, ghastly!
Who would have thought it?
Regulars devoid of grit,
Of nerve, who practiced hard in their land
To chase foxes than men!
I oversaw the burial
That no impious foot or savage
Triumph would stir his peace
Or mauled laurel.
I let no music stand;
Only prayer for a great man.

Washington:

A trench we dug in the road
For his body, blanket-wrapped;
Lowered it cold
Near the site mapped.
We stood round in prayer.
The torch-lights larger
(giving vague dimensions
to the men)
Seemed to light our pale words
Grown sad and small
As though God was all
And we his half-lit world.
Then we moved on, run by events
And rush for profit.
Such scenes make one
Think again and again
Of our boisterous hope,
Its engine germ,
The source of our land,
The rudiment hands
That plough it and till,
Work at what they will
As if for greater dreams
Before some cold sun dips
And age sits
Raveled in those fated to leave,
Not averse, however much the years trot
To slack our surge-driven lot!

Washington:

After this, shall we cackle for relief,
Whine, slump down to the ground,
Fling French goods in grief,
Or snatch 'em from their palms?
I'll not an inch budge
As one fit for regard
As a regular! Stern kinks, whims,
Imprecations spike these war-fouled words —
With mouths, chops cannon-pursed
In field and bayonet ready to smite
Some thick-nosed knight
Or skull split!
Rage alone hosts me
My knot-hole destiny!
Move, then, let us move –
First outward, then within,
With no past gratitude
For laurels won!
Move, 'ere beneath our scudding feet,
Steering ahead straight,
The ground slips
Or limbs grow weak!
Move as with one hectic sound,
Cautious of mettle under heat,
Fearless where we meet
As guns malicious pound
Envious, resentful, yet bidding us to freedom
As good men!

Washington:

Then anew I think of her!
My thoughts stuttering begin to drift,
Falter, as if into a dark mirror
Only to see night lift
In celebration, and her, with hands observant,
Spotted with ink, pulpy wax, made
Fresher in mind
As a sun gained blind.
One can't order the heart
To darken or noon-day soul   ;
As they turn as if more bold   ,
To heal, repair apart.
Soon I dispute within, pine with sense
For Martha, Martha, as words slip
And I more honest
Leap to love her only,
Her good nature lent
So nobly to me.
What a fool at times are we
For love or bullet-hazed country
Who can't express ardor
If not sure.
But my path's straightest
In hers, whatever my surfeit, my flaws.
My honor's safest from assaults
As helped and blessed.
I learn as if quickly my faults
Having slighted her heart.

Washington:

But still there is this war
So close-pressed, intimate, the Ohio campaign,
The march once more
On Duquesne.
I over-brim in confidence
And vex Stanwix to press in my defense,
To plead for me in patriot terms
To Forbes my muted charms:
That I'm not of the common run
Of officers – provincial, narrow
In war, in grief; lax with foes,
Yesterday's backwoods sage under Cain's sun
As if cut out of some fake world
To yield fraud room.
Yet I go nowhere in this hap!
I retire, teased back to habits
Old, practices put off,
That I dare upset.
Only then do I weigh marriage,
Futurity at my age,
The bolt under the heart
To make a new start.
Then swathed in hope over votes
To the House of Burgesses,
Anew I wipe clean the slate
As if of honor, grit,
Knowing human affairs are checkered,
Then to shreds ripped.

Washington:

My challenges are aplenty
At the Mount alone —
I fancy each duty,
Hold each to heart, respire as if from behind some
Stone chalked-marked, or hill, or mountain, each
Day, week, year,
Smarted all the while by hands apace
And heart, stretching to a future with fattened
Crops and slaves who hold, lock
Me in for good
With records scrolled
Beneath some pulsing clock!
But for my ambition
A lot to pay has one.
And what have I of slaves
To keep them reckoned, bound here
But for good rule and will,
My rigor, discipline to steer
Them as if to mightier tasks
Under days that pass!
They are my people, family
Half-defined, come to labor for me!
But I sell them as any planter
And score with ready money
When they are fat and lusty,
With nimble limbs sounder;
Though under one servitude
Each thrall I singly rule.

Washington:

On Sundays, they are loose, free to take on
The ready yield of crops,
Loaded to the ear! Unbridled, free
To cede, sell stock,
Till gardens, turn
Upward as if to face the pendent sun
Or a preying bird; examine what they will
Of grass, of buzzing flies that sail,
Hum from toe to head,
Scud swill,
Or land on some stool
Or plank-bed.
My slaves are free of flogging, small pox,
Penalties rarest made to shock!!
But what of release, liberty, replete with troubles
That our system breeds?
Must we flout heaven with shackles,
Heedless of Moses, that Hebrew King?
And how are we to sift, kill
Bondage, slay evil
When to live here is hopeless
Without their harnessed juice —
Though we know ourselves our decisions
Wrong, our justice ill-starred,
Given to questions amiss, frail offense,
As if cocked to rush inevitable Doom!
Aye, nothing seems true but twice the same
As in a dream unchanged!

Washington:

Has soul answer
Given how This Darkness crawls,
Grows utmost as if to the point of cure,
But intolerable to all?
Have we only vague assurance
Of some cryptic date we advance
In mind and soul? Some tomorrow half-born,
Routed again and again
As if to hold back life to come
And what freemen ought
Feel? Have we this scourge until we adopt,
Vouch from within that all are one —
That liberty be sanctioned, passed on
And bondage wrong?
One's past is strong all the more
Like any past of life that
Is no more
Except for whom the past
Has failed free men. But our past
Conferred wealth, might;
We were reared on that labor,
That reasonable error, myth,
Whose soldered wounds shall never heal,
'tis said, however folks are patient,
Schooled in sense
In degree to zeal.
But for now, we are lost
As shackled limbs reap crops.

Washington:

Likewise, we hug close these fields, these richest
Lands, as if not to let go or give away
Whilst slavery's yelping Hand
Endures each day;
Persists as if a necessity in the court of the
Present, wider to dissent, rife
In the factious future, a changing lesson
That posterity fancies its own.
But in the meantime, we make heavier scales
Appear lighter to our creeds
And judge ourselves by what we need
So as not to fail.
But as sure as death
This will be reckoned with.
But now it's time for marriage,
A warrior's reward!
What call ought I give this change
In me so rash to keep my word?
Who is the guarantor of such delight, such
Happiness except deep down in the heart's
Dark depth, the work of years inward stripped,
Past doubt blotted out.
I'm alone now to speak with her
As if to remove a spectral mask,
A screen within as if from out of the past
That sinks deep the soul.
So much in me is love unsaid
That loads my head!

Ona Judge

What of us?
Who asks about our route,
   Our ancient curse, our dry-bone hope?
Our tongues aren't groomed for verse
Nor lips puffed with poetry
But felled by the pronged triumphs
That we see!

What about us, bare-necked,
Coming back from field,
Under court-appointed whip and sky
That keeps darkening?
What about us asking?

Change and evil,
Sea-crossings and death—
All strange to them!
But what of us, behind the face of things,
As if flickering out of the past, the present?
What of us, black-faced temples
Who can't sing or praise
When muskets ring
And bells blast?

Washington:

A rooster's voice breaks free some days
  that creatures might be happy
  that the Bards of State at table
  may burn a lamp for Abel.
But Time will pass its seal
    what Providence reveals!
In my will I have set limits
        as if by the boundaries of the sun
        on different scales there-from,
        not figured on clocks rusted
        as if fear-prized in men
        whose years will never come!

Ona Judge:

The Lamb of God will round a darker blood,
Will turn the knuckles of Achilles' hand
A deeper red
In Jacob's land.

The deer of Isaac will not leap in vain;
The Romans' javelin will stick in sand.
Graves will open to a scorching sun
And dust will close the gun.

Where evils abound,
Who will cancel bondage for the slave?
Piedmont's Laws will be ripped to shreds,
And planters, stalked like prey.

And all shall be well,
And all shall be well in this land!

Ona Judge:

Washington's married, at peace, takes no look
Backward at his past, his feet forward, imperfect:
'Tis duty at the wheel!
Mary Ball boycotts the wedding, putting him
In mind of her needs equivalent, concluded
Long ago In cold-blooded show.
He assumes a seat in the House of Burgesses.
He serves on committees. He learns
Policy: to hold his tongue,
When to act listener, aggressor,
When to keep his station, shift support,
Surrender to gain the upper hand,
Reap superior-ground, advantage, profit
Against the pulse to fight.
He learns to juggle action, temper brain-ache,
Incline an ear, catch his prey listening, to stay still
When heartfelt, poised to edge in a word or two.
The tongue's a nimble sword, he finds,
A golden knife, heeded and observed
As if to will compromise, assert it
With a snake's delay or fatal bite.

Ona Judge sings:

All's hurrying this General's eye
By shadows to take his stand.
No footprint frightens him,
Nor king's imperial hand
Nor limb of man!

Ona Judge:

But steadily events fret him
As he learns the villainy of Brit merchants
As if hoaxing him, their wobbling conjectures,
Their self-assumptions sanctioning
Greed, guile as if for goods needed, inscribing
Costs higher on crossed-faced planters!
Soon he lags in payments,
Learns to pay as he goes
As if to avoid an enemy, a foe!
The prices for his goods in London
Fire resentment
Tipped as if to the efforts of his agent
As are tobacco prices to punitive rules,
Bearing no face in Virginia, no veritable voice
As if to smite men with compunction, by-pass
Them! Then all crops are adrift on London's flood
As if the whole of that market were fair and true
To meet a planter's need!
The Stamp Act's promptness, the talk of Dr. Warren,
Of Adams — all usher in a new epoch of speech
As if out of reach of mercy, patience.
It's ripe for conscience to cry Liberty,
Cry representation as if too risky
To be mum, mute, with eyes lying!

Ona sings:
What color does your courage sport,
What foam-whipped rock display?
What dream blazes up from dirt?
What farmer dazzles clay?

Ona Judge:

All this comes out of congregations past,
Early meeting halls, selectmen noble
Amongst those who patched clothes, mended
Fences! They laid the footing far back – their
Schooled misgivings, grave doubts —
As if at the bottom and settlement of folk
Who roused dissent! Aye, their grievances —
Decades back — as if reaching the ear identical,
Rousing it, soon give way to causes political,
Menaced strains from a ditch, an alley, a path,
That grip the hand, guide rage in all directions!
Long is the memory of that corporate heart
With its ailments deepened, its injustices,
The want of will to check expenditures,
Of needs that are yet replete
Within the sway of rule!
A reproof from Robert Cary,
His London agent, measures the time in rage,
In local bulletins, leaflets
As if kindling days to come.
Soon after, he's frocked
Head of the Continental Army,
Without forethought, regret,
As if fixed for eternity, light fashioned and bold.
London's fixed bond of unity breaks,
Its decrees of fate wheel like someone else's
In the gritty dust.
Teach me, O Lord, to number my days
That I many apply my heart to wisdom!

Washington:

This rumble in me lies in America,
Too, as if boisterous with the fate of things:
America – open to peoples on every side
As if to distract us, blight our sense of distance!
But this cannot intermit itself, desist from life, put
An end as if to play, our emboldened freedom!
Are we ready for war? The broadest hearts feel
So, asserting rights, our pride as if to light up the
Powder, rouse the surge-tide, the mind-locked
Sea to strike upwards to the coddled heavens!
Are we ready, smooth-tongued minds,
Schooled as if in self-government, to breathe
As if between cellar and clearing,
Wall and trench, as between what's
Not spelled out fully and what's said?
I have spoken so much within, as if in the ooze of
Things, the mire, my draftsman's compass on
Virginia's charts, her maps delineating the proper
Way for my life, sketching subtleties out of want,
Distress, to which there is no other way!
But now my needs within are my countrymen's,
However bitter-tasting war sticks in our throats
And fatigue encroaches on us, ghostlier, freer,
Assisting another's pillared need!
We are work-worn for Freedom, Liberty,
As if wiping clean the British slate
To make way for it like giddy orphans!
And these my thoughts are as a slight
Part of the conceit, of America's reverie,

That will soon become as if under heaven's light
A shaky reflection of resolve, of power, of will
And resolution on which to stamp our purpose.

Washington:

Shall a verse come true,
A promise, a pledge for victory
Become ravenous hope, a fixed end?
Beyond, look, an eagle sails above us, aye,
As if over trees, hills, mountains, crags,
Stretching its hurried wings into space!
Its thrust's unquenched as if by fictive heights,
Storied truths and failures, but
Held cool to our eddying darkness!
No fate can be as unpleasant here
Save subjugation, servitude,
Its muffled dark as if preying on the
Mind's freedom! O the mind!
It grows hard, not easy, to be free, released,
Which comes first to us as strangers,
Only to sink off as if chased, pursued!
It grows hard to be free,
Heavy-eyed, straining, so work-worn at night!
It's easy to wish for less as if in blindness
To continue under a wolfish king, his
Saw-dust throne tilted as at an angle from
Here, absurd with heavier blows of hauteur
And Parliament's arrogant stare!
No! Nothing stands still
To any happening! Nothing!
Every moment is the right one
To make just the law
And what we have left of freedom.
Our foes shall only strengthen us –

Our excellence, our stealth —
Where blows are hardest, most severe;
And when out with lanterns ahead of them,
We'll date them with their deaths.

Washington:

Victory or death, I scroll on paper,
As if to feel the ducking eye
Dodge an end or apt wager
Ere Providence shifts sides
To claim what it will!
Thoughts like measures vie to fill
My brain, aye, grow as if into rival parts
To cull, start
With Ewing and Greene, strict to the second!
They fear no braid of the King's rope
As rock they in Glover's boats
With Knox and Sullivan — all reckoned
With Calwalder for battle,
Bolder than what men tell!!!
Unfazed, we rise, sprint toward Victory,
No noble more than if for freedom,
Nor bounteous than for duty, the fee
For a boatman's crossing.
Our triumphs anew blaze — raw, fearless
Through cold and steepest passes!
Shelter your hearts, I cry, with Caesar's grit –
With blankets, guns you take,
With artillery and horses,
With smell of sweat and weariness!!!
Make way for kelps worse, depths
Without warmth or ration!
Winter's chill's blessed
For foes to kill best!

Washington:

Now we move in the thick
Of it, my men alone —
A hoard of colonies, at best,
As if pumping hope – militia officers,
Artisans, farmers, laborers,
Clerks, an array of them
Ribbed as with iron –
Men of mean dress, with button-less coats,
Worn shirts, breeches that evoke
What crops stacked they or goods
Sold, what trades they knew –
Whether fished they or sowed,
On nets toiled or chopped wood!!
All are mine at my back,
Quickened for hell's attack!

Ona Judge:

Like Pilgrims ankle-deep,
Wading afoot — out of sound,
Their muskets shift
As if on hollowed ground.
The sun on apples, on hay,
On blushing leaves, licks the earth;
Not passion's slave this tongue
But heedful of Nature first,
Her laws of Consequence
That can't from earth shift
Nor breathe an alien Spring.

Washington:

Maddened Boston ignites the war,
Heaving chests of tea
From docked ships
Into the sea
As if for middlemen, smugglers
Alike to prosper, thrive,
Go well with equity
And the East India Company.
Monopoly, possession –
Call it what you will,
But it's our curtained future
Unleashed by high-browed Britain
To follow upon the heels
What Britain feels!
I lament such hubbub stress,
Such inventions of war and method
Down to the populace
Like the mutinous turns of shaft or wheels
Of an engine,
As if making it rise and fall,
Making spins heedful, necessary,
And contrivance free.
We break so much inside
Our worlds, our plough-marked order
As if to create a people better
Whose outcome's but a civic sign,
A mirror as if to proceed with double caution
However the perversion wrong.

Washington:

But I change, shift in this as if before
A firing squad. The bitter
Decree of heinous rule
Makes peace in the heart wither
As with bad fruit —
Then on everything lodge its smell,
Its rank effect —Boston's misfortune
On us all, empty-mouthed, watching!
No, this will not do,
This acute testimony,
The width of tyranny
As horses neigh and cows chew!
Human warmth must twist cold
That free men rage bold.
Soon I'm in Boston.
We're all in Boston
On Lexington's Green!
America's born
As if with muskets, gunshot,
And smooth-tongued orators
Plotting war;
And what we see before
Us, drenched with light,
Doused, sun-blessed
As if with God's scouring fist,
Stays more bright.
Forgotten today is any pain
Or shock of sons slain.

Washington:

A brother's sword is sheathed
In a kinsman's breast;
Peace is cold, bleak,
As if choked, adrift!
Blood's spilled;
Fields are bared.
The windows of Boston,
Blacked out, numb.
Hate creeps into a neighbor's yard—
One a Tory, the other patriot.
Anger outweighs thought.
Even the sky is hard.
Muskets bleat out the hate of men
Or rage begun.
But unity must be most upper
Amongst us; no irresolution
Ought tilt us from one side or the other
To addle action.
I believe Gates and Lee
Catch in me
Less than they look for,
Yet cling as if to my grade in fear.
Of loyalty, they are bustling born,
But of self-interest more,
Deeming victories for sure
 Belong to them o'er me.
But I live with such poison
And swap it, strengthened.

Washington:

When Congress takes charge of Boston,
Its troops in Roxbury,
I'm loud as a wind's roar
To include me.
Men sharpen their knives,
Hug wives
Knowing to more fiery ventures
They'll be sent
As if to annul bondage,
Shatter it,
Rend its
Maggot-rope in rage.
These events I follow
As if to Himalaya go.
Bunker Hill's a victory of sorts
For hare-eyed Brits. They count
A thousand dead
And reflect
On the carnage, the slaughter,
Turning over
Dead men on their backs –
The price of their attack.
That evening, with lanterns lit,
Howe sees the triumph was a palm too costly;
His boots, blood-soaked, wading Victory,
Had smothered it.
I am off to Cambridge first
To assume the role I sought.

Washington:

We scout about, search for 18,000 men –
Numbers, an essential condition
Of war, as with bread and cannon
To gain a fitting end.
The camp's lice-filled, spare,
As if to suffer in —
With dug latrines, hay, manure, excrement
About fields near stinking tents!
The site looks washed ashore:
Shacks made of boards, sail-clothe;
Others of stone, turf, brick,
Or of any plant chopped for shelter.
We work as if to gut squalor,
Then quarantine soldiers.
Deception I rely on,
As if pitching to bring the Brits to
Reckon I'm theirs, one
Foreseen true.
This deep-eddying ruse steers me
Steadfast, as if true as much as I settle
On duty. We're outnumbered
But not out-witted.
Two generals are amongst my best,
Knox and Greene, as much as any
Soldiers who look on at me
Point-blank in trust.
They are safe-guards
With strong hearts.

Washington:

Soon the Brits quit Boston!
Hastened as if tenant-farmers —
Rats in haste! They scour, run,
Scuffle as if mauled, trounced by curs.
Bunker Hill had stranded them,
Shriveled their blood-fringed handling
Of it, its dark horror, marking
Off the dead from the seamy living.
And I striding feel joyous, untaxed!
One-day bells will ring out —
Bonfires blaze – and men will shout
That the wheezing Brits gulped our axe.
They leave dockyards, as if from an abyss,
Bloated with Tories swelling ships.
In all, I assume the soldier,
Aside the citizen:
Fixed to that brief honor
I bear that end
However fueled by ambition
Or another tongue
O'er-brimming with laced praise
Today
To scratch my name in dirt
Or write a poem of me —
Of my gallantry
Reckoned first.
I share my country's stake,
But service first.

Ona Judge:

Henry Knox at ease looks back,
armed with Franklin's hammer,
to smash the shanty wood
of George's manor.

Behind a scaffold platform,
the Ghost of a killer
struts through Putnam's dreams,
ringing trees with murder.

O what mystery is hate
Like mighty war,
A hand without a mate!

I'm made out of Words, sir,
but stones are just as hard.
I'm one who greets such stones
to rate them good or bad.

But must I laud the good today
or wring dry the bad?
I've known my kitchen feet to trudge
on battlegrounds as hard.

Poor me! I must contend with hate
as in my Bible's past
where words are as hard as stone,
to satisfy and last.

Ona sings:

Poor Turlygod! Poor Tom
Out of his mind today;
His butcher friend gone,
Drowned in clay
The Tories say!

When the sun comes up
For the vomit-mouthed
With smallpox,
The wind is hot
And blood's on a flagpole
From soldiers shot!

They sing aloud, "Be good to us!"
As shots for blood resume
And boast of "Redcoats" in the grave
To yield each Yankee room.

Can you see what a body's like,
Tory and Rebel alike?
Your lips blew out the flame!
Whither shall go I,
Equipped with drowsing pain
To endure the planter's lie.

Washington:

Then on to New York, but not
Before black men enroll, reenlist —
Their courage bested at each stretch,
Their vouchers, lion-mettled
And ready as if to sound loudest in time!
Their pledged labor astounds, stuns us,
Ringed by daylight
And hectic night!
They stride as if behind lines
In the winter icebound, the short-lived spring,
Ne'er scripted for rubble reward
Or battles cancelled.
I see them brave, true, still, strong,
Backs unbent and iron wills.
Every inch a man, these men! And yet
When I stare captive, I see immeasurable
As if over my eyes an unraveled whim
Of history, a freak at the wheel,
And we milk-limbed, grappling fools,
Ever eager to indulge
Good practice at will
For some crop to grow
At their cost! 'Let it not be,' I say!
But it must to survive, prosper!
There's no random debate here
Shredded as if for my footing to stay.
Huddled as in a planter's cell,
This scourge tricks all.

Ona Judge:

Write a future to step in
that cancels doubt
painted with a sign
that leaves Ona out!

Take something from her
she never knew she had
from the end of each century,
to keep her Jesus bad.

Then take her salutations
that edge the eye with hope,
seditious as her failures
that hold so much revolt.

Eeny, Meeny, Miny, Mo,
catch a helot by the toe
if she hollers let her go
and your soul, soul, soul
soulless soul!

O that wild beast he cites again
As if in Canaan among Puritan!
A yoke to government, both sacred and civil,
Blights no pact with ancestral rebel!

Washington:

On watch, we count the battles —
New York, first! The Whispers come
As if to gnaw the soul —
That I've ten thousand only
And a third sick! 'Quit yourselves
Like men,' I shout. My small-sword's out as if
To flaunt gore, Victory, brandish it as if a tribute
From site to site before half-rigged troops!
What wrath can be tested, what mettle
Proved of Old Put? How many brave fellows
Must one lose? This I quarrel
Nights within for Posterity's sake to choose!
But life's testing
I fear comes 'ere my time!
Be that right, such questioning? All must
Face such terror, mad heights
Of risk, of fear drawn as if from dreadful nights,
Leaving little light.
No different am I from others
Only all that's living for
Is at stake, however carved-out pain
Under the heart's more than hate.
But we must rouse, stir, haul grit through mud
As if for every hope that mounts us!
No folly's more costly than mistrust,
Hoodlum fear, a heart folded-up!
But want of confidence is not ours
That men feel each hour.

Ona Judge:

We're not alone on this earth
To tremble in this den
Where light's darkened like gas
And heaven's' stars are tin.

We're not alone in this grief,
To hold Apocalypse back
Where the seeds of time are crackling
In a shifting sky of black.

We're not alone in this pit
Like dogs who squirm and stink,
Whose victories are in place
To fit some planter's speech.

All the while we stand and pray —
Poor wretches we,
Our chary presence
With our gallantry.

Ona sings for Hercules:

His teeth! Sir Washington's got his teeth!
Watchdogs bark as good men speak!
Whose gums be sore this coming week?

Washington:

But I'm held so to rebuke, to censure,
As if from assaults within! Who'd expect
Five warships up the East River,
Bold-struck, roaring northward
As if to coax, wheedle as decoys
Hessian play?
They fight as in costumed darkness
As if in the devil's dress!
How we are stricken, beaten down,
Impaled against trees!
Some on knees slackened
Are shot or strapped to cannons!
I patrol on horseback
As if to staunch attacks.
I learn soon enough
The pace of their army
From light into dark,
As if with footsteps nearest me.
Then we take flight!
We must to New Jersey; make retreat,
As if trembling from the fate
Of things! Move in haste,
With the terror of comrades shot,
The sick and cold
Doubling the load
From the chase of British talk!
Nothing is aptly said
To raise our heads!

Washington:

Cold, cold was that crossing —
Bitter, bitter
That winter chill coming
Against the glare
Of men, field-stripped and thin!
What went wrong in Manhattan?
At the heights, at Harlem?
At Chatterton's Hill, at Fort Washington?
No need to crouch idly
As if over a map? I was there!
My expertise useless to me
As if only to breathe in the air
Of rout to the Delaware! But I'll avenge
This black event!
And the arrogance of them! On our rivers
Swelling our numbers dead!
Are we to squat in horror,
Fold hands, shrink, cower, bow heads
As they guest-cover the earth,
Fill with music our curse?
Damn them repairing our ready forts
As if to keep them ripe for Court
And King! I'll not long become
Feeble to this,
Breaking ice to bits,
On the run!
I'll rout this defeat
Or swell a vengeance deep!

Washington:

Later at Trenton
We cut the earth as if in half.
'For God's sake, keep by your officers,'
I shout, I blast
To have an effect on them,
From striplings to men.
The Hessians are caught off guard
As if contriving a time to rush, charge.
Then Cornwallis I put a-running —
Devil-driven, chased, puffing over
Frost-covered twigs; the chill of a blade
On him, my short-lived speech!
Let him go unbuttoned now and raw
To match what he saw!
No love for Tories, I say.
Let 'em lift their measling feet, defect,
Run, but leave us their night-shirt space
For troops to rest,
Be fed by tent-flaps,
Vacant barns or shacks
Where mouths can chew morsel
And meat scrap!
I'm never done, never alone!
Providence has led much
For me, for us
As if to haul us richer home
To victory! I'm named general
Against sullied battles.

Washington:

And fealty? Trust? Who needs
It more than bitter foes
Behind whose doting backs the unseen
Smite men cold!
But how often we are wrong,
Muscled more good than strong,
Nursed as if to know sure trust
Than cunning lust.
But a traitor, twined
Like a snake in bed,
Breasting blood-sucking head
On us, our charge, runs Grief's pain
Furthest into hearts,
Lost and dark.
This I suffer from Arnold
Who betrayed me,
Graced with medals once, now gross dog
Feeding fleas;
Who wiped clean his slate of trust
For gold — this greed-flushed
Cur Incarnate! I wish him shot,
Bleached-out, hacked to death!
No need for mercy here,
Whose demi-devil darkness
As if in us, ever-mute distress,
Is never for healing clear.
Not when one scraps country
For money!

Washington:

Then we've Lafayette!
Not even a son, but diamond son,
Baring grit
Under tent-flaps, raised guns!
His loyalty, hard-faced to the cause,
Rallies valor abroad,
Culled with honor, ready money,
Whetting hope for the country!
This kin to Arnold's underworld
Like loftiest heaven to hell!
But Arnold won't rest to kill,
To lap guilt in swill!
I myself will run a blade through him
To breach his hungry skin!
But we never catch him!
I send spies, assassins
To New York, culled men
Bid to kill him,
But he escapes anew—
His leprous separation
Over ready waves
With British knaves!
Be gone, cur! Be gone, traitor,
White-faced demon to your country men!
Be gone from this home,
Its settled peace, its ruddy splendor!
Never come back, never, never
To enter the realm of soldier!

Washington:

The rot is ever here of traitors,
Perfidious fiends reared in malice
Past sleep, terror! Their Judas-chore
Awakens stress,
Edgy affliction, distrust,
Adversities they suck best,
These rat-shadows bloody
For money!
So many betray, lie
Awake to exploit, beguile a country
To despoil what they see
'Ere they evilly die.
Arnold was no less, no more than one
Monstrous fiend of Adam.

What now do we see?
I see many such creatures
On steps empty climbing,
Racing as if hastened mutineers,
As if freemen steep in pain,
Never-resting by pith of change,
Of wonder, life, freedom
To grasp what we govern.
'Tis a dream, a fantasy? What was
Our daring feat? Valley Forge?
Kip's Bay? Some queer
Spell laid elsewhere? War's
Law of requital, repay,
Cashiered more ruthless than all?

Ona Judge:

How high the platform-conscience, how high the
Apple branch? It is worth a candle flame in the
Distance? What of Consequence, Sir, when
Interiors are cold and men crack open a skull
For imperial show? I clap my hands in praise and
Fill the sky with song whether I face a gallows or
Or heart once strong.
But think of this small light
When the General's eye is dead
And evening with its scent
Is black above his head.

Sin boldly, they say! But against self or prey?
Against want or deficiency to swallow up the day?
But what of murder, betrayal, some hurt of the mind
When hate eats it up or conscience sits blind?
Does the Master in good stead stand?
Must he adjust again to Bondage, the Hangman's
Curse, as citizen? "But what of family,
The country's oneness?" he cries
As guilt begs innocence with cunning breath.
Yet evil still it is that freedom doesn't bring
As we trek each Golgotha before perishing.

Washington:

I prate to myself, talk, speak
As if franchised to outsmart,
Cull conceit,
From a maimed heart.
But the Forge — how stark, how dark
That Valley at every moment more dark,
Worse for virtue, food, mercy,
Turning minds to frenzy!
How does one liken hunger
To raw savagery
Or both to cruelty?
Whose scummy aim is fiercer?
From Cain downward we discover
All stand ruthless to savage hunger.
But camp we set up as best
We can after Morristown,
After Brandywine, Burgoyne's defeat
To shut things down!
What else had I to do with dysentery
Afoot, frostbite, typhus, scurvy,
With men devoid of soap, shoes,
Made worse by bad news.
For want of blankets they froze,
Their minds turning inward in thought
Toward victory, a warm cot
Or what they chose.
My ground was slipping and all
Beneath me to hell.

Washington:

Was that not pain enough, agony? What more
For America? What more! But we rose
From disorder,
Edged by discipline
With von Steuben's arm of effort—
The fires he roused best
To duplicate and redouble with will
What victory feels.
'Give me time,' he tells me,
'One glimpse of hope a day;
I'm closer to victory
Than Caesar displayed.'
Then I knew Providence would hustle this cause
Or from this end toss us....
But still for the French waiting, waiting!
So senseless it was, too,
Vouching nothing
But patience, bad news,
Gossip, the hearsay of talks,
The speed of ships
North and south! I thought   .
New York best to make an end of it!
I knew the task,
Am clever,
A winner,
A master of craft.
But no winds grumbling waken ships
More than dauntless hearts!

Washington:

One is left troubled, too,
By slaves deferred among black men free!
Can one separate the two
As free men work? Rhode Island sees
What I miss when travelling deeper,
Repairing black soldiers
From the sightless South. These share
The same air we breathe,
Says Laurens: Free men
With sure footing who raise guns with us,
Are decked in the same cloth,
Have like foes rushing them!
But the work force is meager,
Sparse, we say, if they rise freer.
Still we wait for the French, wait the
Gathering storm in quiet accord, wait with
Calid hope swallowed down.
THEN nightmares are less —
We learn they're docked off Newport,
Rochambeau and his ready court!
Then De Grasse with no need of roads —
His sails pumped free to Yorktown and bold!
These lift my spirit,
Just sighting them!
Were the dates mere accidents
To bring up men?
My fires seemed burnt out, charred logs
Swaddling Death's doubt.

Washington:

Then that Penury that plagued mind and heart
Is no more! NO MORE! As if on a ledge
I stood. The sea pulsed,
My doubts ripped to shreds!
I strip fear to the skin,
Rip out its carcass-lining,
Its inner dread
Never to load my head!
Coy Cornwallis waited
For his reinforcements. Clinton hedged.
They fought in redoubts, spiking cannons, guns,
Shuffling, lunging forward to withdraw from
Trenches, empty them, run! Then the fields fell
Silent and a flag flapped white.
The toll of that Victory: Fields paved with
Bodies, black and white, a grave of one vast
Smell with arms sticking up and rotting limbs
Like plants to fill hell;
War's dark-light of terror
With creaking barrows
Rutting the limp earth
To sweep fields clean!
Cornwallis's deputy presents his sword.
He couldn't himself, so contemptuous of me.
Lincoln, my deputy,
Accepts it to Yankee Doodle's word.
Then it ended! We sheathed swords,
Cheered – dirty, ragged, bold!

Ona's Song for Veterans:

Have you something for these soldiers
Felled at Yorktown,
Wearing a badge of courage
On this stone-dressed ground?

Have you something for these soldiers
To come to terms with them,
Their death for their country
Against the bugler's hymn?

Ona Judge's rebuke:

Make ready the clanging!
Fetch the prophet's Psalm
For slaves who've ceased to wait
For counterfeit balm!
Can birds resume the egg?
Can Men the womb
Or Eden recommence
The divine tune?
Wait an' see, wait an' see!
The searchlight beam is bright
As muskets jerk
And twitch for Light!

Ona Judge on the Middle Passage:

Sharks look aside each other
Rolling the dead who drowned,
Marked without names or faces
Fathoms down.

Who are these kin cast off,
Added to the sea,
Sunk down to sleep and death,
Too brave for pity?

Who are these Passage-brethren
Locked under Adam's sin!
No camp is of any defense
Too great for Eden.

——— ——— ——— ——— ——— ——— ———

No wounded angel plies the steel!
No threats to God in heaven!
The seraphim are silent still
As Vattel's Hamilton,
Cloud-capped Jefferson
And all of Eden.

Washington:

All that follows is more new!
Muskets gut their mark,
Words like milk and honey
Trickle down the dark.
We negotiate, we see   *Ona Judge:*
With Congress the heft of slavery,
States rights kindling minds   *'In vain does the*
To blunt, blur in time.   *Watchman keep vigil.'* There's
In all, the good of Law-   *Wrath under his heart as if*
And -Arms is enshrined.   *Grace, stripped from his soul,*
Law's more sacred each time   *dissolved into. parts!*
Than civil war.   *'If the Lord doesn't build*
And no one'll choke on meddling King *the House,*
When bells ring.   *in vain do its builders labor.'*
                                                  The limits of their strength

We are free, reaching out   *discard their prayer.*
Spirit-stirring as if to the sun, our brim-full star
To uncover the route   *'In vain is your early rising,*
Of that year   *your going down to rest.'*
Seventeen seventy-six!   *Under artillery fire,*
So long as liberty's fixed   *which side do you bless?*
And Nature's God doth come   'Woe unto the world
To bring men home,   *because of offenses; for it must*
We are free, Hamilton!   *needs be that offenses come,*
Free, Jefferson!   *but woe to that man by whom*
Remember this mother-root creed   *offences come,'*
With Knox, Putnam, and Greene!   *too late for balm.*

POST SCRIPT:

WASHINGTON TO ONA JUDGE:

This Thing of Darkness, aye, this bondage —
This I acknowledge, divvying me up in darkness!
'Tis never unacknowledged, un-avowed.
But I temper it — the absolute, the arbitrary,
The power willful over others,
The power to kill at any time –
This I temper!
And our surrender to Silence,
Its dust in a windy street,
Chewing into expunged voices, breasts,
Saw-toothed into ribs, looting lawful hearts,
The slaves' maddened hope!!
This I temper!

But what choices had I
Beyond historic law where
Ghosts echo still? Beyond expedience,
The effort to render each his due
As future-seers overlay this show,
This receipt of utility?
But without strength to curb might, Justice is little,
Is but a shot thundered in sleep,
A ghost beckoned, a hapless shade,
Dispersed like smoke into any wind
Without force to second it, abet it,
Stand with it with iron arms
For bondmen, helots, vassals
And wrath to come.

O what part is never told,
What part is severed, rent wide open —
Ever opening to the rest!
What liable skin of a man's hide
Is beaten still, whip-oppressed
To parading shadows!
You know, I know the spectacle,
What past is never seen,
What sound of treading feet
Trampling, unbidden, alarmed by watchmen
Is never gone! What veiled yoke
Downward into darkness
Is mine still flaring,
That seeks an argument, a dispute,
A stranger devil to wound!

O the darkness of it all, the wantonness contained,
That I am mad, too, a self-dared fool to
Enact a blood-ceased moment, a variant future,
                a grant to your gift of blood
                    where Minutemen stood!

POST-POST SCRIPT:

ONA JUDGE TO WASINGTON:

But still headlong nothing! Into nothing! Our
Desolation, blank to you! Our dirt-veined feet!
On blood-fields! Blood-oceans! Nothing!
Teeth torn out! Hides lashed, flogged! Salt ground
Into wounds! Silence! Silence! Names erased!
Gullets slashed! Throats! Nothing!
You with your gloves of henchmen's cloth!
A face without eyes! Knuckle-white! Silence!
Blows with a paddle! Sawed off legs!
Chopped toes! Cracked bones! Silence! Salt pork,
Cornbread rotted! Blood-blest meat! We –
Maimed, charred, trampled! Silence!
With your fixed prices like celebrant
Snouts overhead! We face downward to shun it,
The horror! The alarm! The raid out of darkness!
Devil-crime of Patriot pride!
Slave, Black — same tag! Demon-label!
Nothing! Nothing! Bloody welts! Brocade flesh,
Marked hide! Work-camp muscle! Soul-trashed!
Under a lynching tree!

Ona Judge's Song for Black Veterans
of the Revolutionary War

Let us now praise famous men,
Black men aflame, grown mightier
On battlefields, in struggles doomed,
Who'd breathe their last sigh to fight
Than give Oppression room!

The Redcoats on their shoe-black paths,
The Redcoats beaten down,
Crossed their Hausa guns,
The jingling of their spurs —
    Their steeds on yielding ground
    Heralding the dawn.

Find room in a song for them
In the gong of a bell's din
When Freedom's song is knelled.
The barrel of their musket's still
To gunshot and drill.
Find room in a song for them
Who half-filled hell.

Ona Judge to Master Washington (to herself):

I was thinking what you said, sir!
That's all. About our flight from time,
The rise of sun on Sukey's face
And moonlight on Paine's rhyme.
That's all, sir! A hiding place of sorts
With the clock on the wall that sees
Change coming to Virginia,
And me, hung from a tree.

The heart's that way
When the heart feels hurt.
So rough on the bones
In a servant's shirt.

Take a keepsake, sir:
The crest off a Scotsman's cape?
Or the print of a dog barking blood,
Its rope stiff and straight?
Make it work, sir! Make it work
Where terror rears a tomb.
Tomorrow is the daylight sun
Of Byzantium.
The inky black of night will go
And the cold ring of guns
In your room.

Ona Judge to Master Washington (singing to herself):

The title of the earth isn't white, sir, nor red!
Hiccup on my diamond head!
Hey ragman, touchy thing,
That's how Ona sings.
Like my blanket of deer pelt?
Your burnt-out eyes are suffering.
O show me snots with blood stains,
A handkerchief that bleeds in pain!
The shark-breath of your forehead-thoughts
Are soul-stuffed with the guts of moths!
My suffragette's with another man.
I want them in a rubber band.
That's my song for hung ham.
Like it, sir? You get my drill.
I'm no rat on squirrel hill.
Just your servant in this swill
To laud in Praise House
And crack your rule.

Ona Judge's Second Dream:

The balmy mist of Boston's winter
Is burning through the trees.
Ice loosens, puddles shine
And swallow light-struck leaves.

Flinging up my wave-swine thoughts,
As if huddled in a trench
Behind a hangman's knot
I crouch on a wooden bench.

Workmen unloading cotton bales
Are flooded with the sun
In praise of thy kingdom, Lord,
Like the wives of Solomon.

The yellow eye of Hancock's gun
That blasts my shackled feet
Like ancient Gehenna
Is copied in the street.

Ona Judge's 13 CIVIL WAR Prophesies:

1.
I am no Shadowy Prophet six thousand years ago!
I summon what I see from the shadows of time,
From Degradation to spluttered rhyme!

War flows like a fiery wind here!
That's the Lord's judgment, His redemptive raid,
A fiery breeze that blots the air
To rescind the soldier's blade.

O frightened men with war-patched hands,
Pursue a path more ample!
The height of Sinai's stony crest
Where Jacob rests
Rears a blasphemous temple!

Beside a helmet, a soldier,
Reckoning Apocalypse,
Grips an Angel's plume
From Jerusalem
Where every gate is pearl
In a wood-smoked room.

2.
Outside I watch from a Yorktown bunker;
My heart war-wearied reeks.
The bombs I think are thunder;
My breath, Elijah's speech.

A musket cocked to yield a drop
Is all that blood can stop
As ranks of soldiers march
And lead balls leap and drop
By Degradation's Rock.

————————————————————————————————

Who makes the rounds to close their eyes?
Crack your knuckles, fingers chapped!
Do it with Njinga's ire
Down to a mouse trap!

I'll play the part, Mr. Shopkeeper,
Where death is lived through!
Bring up the bodies put to sleep!
With a voice or groan I'll do it
To retain the rights they keep!

3.
Some fancy what they doubt most
As if to wheel round and round a mine cart
On tracks abandoned that glitter still,
Or upward roll a rock of rubble
Like Sisyphus on Hades' hill.

Time was good to Henry Knox
For hauling cannon on ox-team sleds;
Was cruel to Arnold, pounding flesh
With rubber heels to reach his wife
And salvage self-respect.

Before us now floats a face of flint,
Washington's, seated with Quaker friends,
With outline hard like Caesar's front,
Enlarged hands, gracious among men
To make a name on their tongues.

Once out of war, as battles recede,
Washington's steed is saddled,
Noosed in reins to run.
Soldiers cool their guns.
Washington arises on every front.
Dust scrubs the sun.

4.
The moon-eyed woman's grief
Is scant in Randolph's mind
Like scrap in heaps about his yard
Or chaff at cutting time!

Angels sift through stricken cities,
With speckled hooks-for-meat.
The corpse of an uneaten body
Lies patient in the street.

Blood spurts from a House slave,
The stench of rape stinking!
Can one grudge her rage,
Awaiting the bleeding?

A blow to the head where hate abounds!
Are those His lips wetting the ground?
Are those His palms
Without a sound?

O Moses in my holy mouth,
You shook a king to bits!
My words are Jeremiah's sparks;
Isaiah's off my lips!

5.
I groan, Lord, with the Hebrews,
          but prophets may be late.
    Cotton grows like silver here
      shot through with iron weights.

Bloodshed trails their hoof-beats,
      where Angels drop their wings;
the anchored of them savage,
          the bravest of them, kings.

America's baring herself, her Specter,
          where Killing Angels move
to dwindle like a shadow,
          a Ghost within a groove.

My prayers step off into heaven
            like Travelers in the night.
You are good and forgiving, Lord,
            within this Room of Light.

But men quit their kitchen fires
        for Truth and right to tell
        for such reckoning
      and Abel's right to kill.

6.
Dig up the gold of Richmond,
Under columns white!
Gut its squealing flame,
Its knife-point light,
Once oath-enforced and right!

Tear down its sign of bondage!
Tear it down, its crackling hate,
Its rattle in the wind
By Jacob's gate!

Unrig these velvet realms —
States with law-trashed Rights,
Patterned with a ribbon
Like grass on thickest ice
To bind a nation right!

I know my Redeemer lives
Where the walls of Jericho stood
Where the axe had left its mark
On rotten wood
And disappeared for good!

7.
Dirty stars in the brain
A cold Antietam train
Opens in the rain.

The moon that watches on its side
Watches soldiers crawl in pain
As blood-clots comb their brains.

The wagon trains are strange to watch,
Each ghostly wheel that death turns round
As bloody puddles shroud the ground.

Dirty stars in the brain
Why stuff the earth with drool and pain
And skeletons that weigh like grain?

O Jesus Lord, your ugly wounds
Mock the world we blight!
Speed the blade that sups on Light!

8.
Don't separate the dead,
Farmers, tradesmen!
Sack them in balm —
Stale eyes, broken heads,
Bathed in army lead!

Don't separate the dead,
Black, white, or red,
The ranks of brethren —
Guts balled-up in a ditch,
War the color of this!

Safe in their coffins as if in Trenton,
Soldiers shift from side to side
To share each other's dark —
The rage of Job
Thy breath blew back
As if against the cold.

Their blood cries out from the ground, Lord,
Where Washington has passed;
No boots on top of the soil
Weightier than the last,
Just smoke and mist
To aggravate the grass.

9.
By whitewashed sheds near beaches
Or slave-pens streets away,
He hawked his field-hand chattel
To average out the day.

Now he's dead by daffodils
Where slavers can't be heard,
A well-remembered son
Who scoured the business world.

.

But big-eyed frogs near-by
Like rats infesting grain
Riot by his stone
On which kin bled his name
And riot by the sod and muck
That feel the same.

But who be he, what be he
Behind his bone-house mask,
Behind the heft of his thong
Rotting in the grass?

Woe the swelling joints, the fiery phlegm where
Ranks of prophets stand without a knowing hymn!
But thou, O Lord, art a shield about us,
Our glory and the lifter of our heads!

10.
Make Peace our trodden Path!
Scroll freedom in the dirt!
Wash vomit from our shackles
With a trader's shirt!

Age Bondage to its end
From London to Cape Hope!
It's beautiful to shout aloud
And scorch a planter's coat!

Who will sink the trader's ship,
The Zong man's whip and rod?
A deacon from the parish says,
When God stops killing God.

———————————————————————

She wrote on a Gospel wall,
A wall in Jerusalem;
She wrote on a wall of rain
Through which a wind came.

She cut a lamb in two,
Sucked blood off its cheek;
From sand below a tide
She raised Elijah's feet.

A wind howls in her soul,
The maelstrom of three wraths,
The weight of Yahweh's Word
Who rolled an ocean back.

11.
Rejoice not over me, O Masters
In soap-white suits!
Though I'm in bonds, I shall arise
And follow the road to Jerusalem
Whose Judgment is swift and given.

The Lord will stir up my cause,
Will fetch me forth to Light
Above the time-stricken night
Where no need there'll be of passage,
Half-way or middle, or heaving sea,
And Justice shall shine bright

For these Irons stir,
These groans arouse
A shrewder Host,
A darker grace
When deep winds rock
The stripes on our backs
And chain-ringed legs.

13.
A stone apiece; no race can match that,
A red bristle along the road, an ebb, neap tide,
Abel's enchantment in black,
To lure the Red Sea back.

We'll soon be upon God at death, they say here,
The privilege to split the atom –
Though the soul in yellow dust
Is a new soul steeped in trust
Where the Steeple door is shut
And the Lord's hand takes hold of judgment,
Connecting absence with absence,
Light with light,
Shadow with shadow and light
        from the sole of the foot to the head.
When we meet at death, who will be more dead,
                        O women of Moab,
Blasted by the East wind sprung up,
The wind of many minds sniffed out, many hearts
                        bruised and stricken,
The wind that Uriel screened, curtained under
                    slanting smoke, the wind of
A pile of seeds slumped up against wounds,
        a revelation, a mother-root Epoch
                    of war-tormented sons?
Maranatha, she cried. Maranatha!

LOVE strikes the heart to reach the Foe
That ranks with grief and other woes,
The dread of judgment in the soul.
Even dying snakes can crawl.

Loosely drawn from characters, data
in **THE PAPERS OF GEORGE WASHINGTON,**
The University of Virginia Press; **Mount**
Vernon portraitures; **David McCullough's**
1776; Alan Taylor's *THE INTERNAL ENEMY;*
Harold Bloom's OMENS AND MILLENNIUM;
THE LITURGY OF THEHOURS; "Fannie Lou
Hamer and the refusal to compromise,"
Stephen Carter, The Veritas Forum, 2016;
Edward Lengel's GENERAL GEORGE
WASHINGTON, and Theodore Weld,
Angelina Grinke, and Sarah Grinke's
AMERICAN SLAVERYAS IT IS: TESTIMONY
OF A THOUSAND WITNESSES, among
many other primary and secondary
sources to create this historical fiction.

James Wm. Chichetto, C.S.C., is a priest-scholar
and a professor of Communications at Stonehill
College, North Easton, Massachusetts, USA.
He has been published over 300 times and is the
author of 11 books of poetry, including BLOOD
ACCOUNTS and DREAM OF NORUMBEGA,
Bk.VI, from which some of the poems of this
drama have been taken. The publication
of his work has been aided by NEA and NEH grants
as well as by other academic, literary honors.

Cover art for this book: J. Wm. Chichetto